1974

This book may be kept

Dostoevsky in 1860 on his return from Siberia

TO MANYA
Quae dum vivit vivo

Dostoevsky and Existentialism
with reflections on
"The Grand Inquisitor"

by
Albert Douglas Menut

Coronado Press 1972

Published by
Coronado Press
Box 3232
Lawrence, Kansas 66044

SBN 87291–044–X

Manufactured in the USA

Publisher's Note

Thirty years ago I was a graduate student of Dr. Albert Douglas Menut, taking my M.A. degree under his direction.

After years of silence, and fond memories on my part, we somehow re-established communications with each other. I did not hesitate to solicit from Dr. Menut some work of his which I might publish. I now have the most unusual opportunity— to pay him my respects, at the same time that I cater to my own good fortune, by publication of this present work.

John E. Longhurst

Contents

Dostoevsky and Existentialism

TODAY in Existentialist circles no name is more universally revered than that of Dostoevsky. Along with his contemporary, the impassioned Danish theologian Kierkegaard, he shares equal honors in the Existentialist Pantheon. Still regarded in his native Russia as a spokesman for the underprivileged, Dostoevsky is hailed in the West as the literary progenitor of the Existentialist *Weltanschauung*. Are the proponents of this bold new therapy for the treatment of the human predicament justified in asserting that Dostoevsky was an Existentialist — precursory, of course — and if this claim can be maintained, what manner of Existentialist was he and to what degree? That a writer endowed with an imagination so vigorous and so prolific should remain patiently constant to a unilinear and unvarying concept of human existence would be strange indeed. Yet this is precisely the impression most likely to be gained from the insistence with which the Existentialist advocates have stressed the central importance of the Underground Man, unquestionably the most original but surely not the only existentially oriented of Dostoevsky's multitude of characters.

It is easy to understand this emphasis upon the Underground Man, for in a hundred passages of his coarse-textured prose this querulous, peevish, splenetic, perverse, penetratingly lucid and triumphantly ambivalent character expresses in the most highly concentrated manner imaginable the sentiments and the cogitations that correspond to the existentialist image of human life. For example:

> "My enjoyment was from the too intense consciousness of my own degradation, it was from feeling that I had reached the last barrier, that it was horrible, but that it could not be otherwise; that there was no escape — that I could never become a different man; that even if time and faith were still left me to change into something different, I would most likely not wish to change, or even if I did wish to change, I could do nothing. Because, perhaps in reality, there was nothing for me to change into."

Is it not already perfectly clear that Dostoevsky's first distinctive novel, *Notes from the Underground*[1] (more correctly translated *Diary written in a Basement*), completed in 1864, was predestined to become the example par excellence, the *locus classicus* of literary existentialism, to be cited time after time by critics and philosophers of a later generation as the prototype of the anxious man, the

---

1. Unless otherwise noted, quotations from Dosteovsky's works are cited from Davaid Magarshack's English translations, published by Penguin Classics.

perplexed man, the resentful and self-deceiving man, whose predicament, long ignored in traditional philosophy, has become the central issue of both Christian and secular Existentialism? For the temper of existentialist thought of whatever variety — whether ancient or modern, Christian, agnostic or atheistic, literary or formally theoretical — tends to be pessimistic. Why should this be so?

The answer is quite simple. The existentialist philosopher concentrates his attention upon *la condition humaine,* upon the situation of the individual man responding to the unpredictable contingencies of life as lived, or existence as existence. In this respect, Existentialism stands in sharp contrast with the major systems of traditional philosophy, where the central issue has always been to discover the first principles of natural law, to determine objectively the typical nature of mankind in general, what ultimately makes man what he is. It describes human nature in terms so general that they might apply to all men everywhere. Aristotle, for example, asserted that man differs from the other animals in that he is the unique *animal rationale.* The foundation of the Cartesian system is Descartes' assumption that reason is the most generally distributed characteristic of mankind. Therefore reason is an essential attribute of all men, an intrinsic factor in human nature, without which man is no longer man. Maybe so, says the Existentialist; but what about the lapses from reason that afflict some of us most of the time and most of us some of the time? In human experience a multitude of situations arise that defy rational solution, and very often we have to choose a course of action *au hasard,* without benefit of ratiocination. Of this yawning gap between the established norms of man's nature — his essence, in professional parlance — and the accidental character of his day-by-day actions the Underground Man was strongly aware. "You see, gentlemen," he says, "reason is an excellent thing, but reason is nothing but reason and satisfies only the rational side of man's nature; while will is a manifestation of the whole life, that is, of the whole human life and all the impulses. And although our life, in this aspect, is often worthless, yet it is life and not simply extracting square-roots. What does reason know? Reason knows only what it has succeeded in learning... and human nature acts as a whole... and even if it goes wrong, it lives."

For the Existentialist, the awareness of our deviation from the norm, from the ideal established as desirable, this marks the beginning of man's unhappiness. The psychological manifestations of this awareness are various, but all the manifestations are uniformly unpleasant, though in greatly varying degrees. First in order of importance is the emotional state of anxiety, which affects all of us some of the time and most of us much of the time. Why are we anxious? We are anxious because we fear to make decisions, the crucial decisions required for the maintenance of our physical being. We are anxious because, as finite beings, we are constantly exposed to physical annihilation. We are anxious because we fear alienation from our environment, estrangement from that to which we properly belong. This anxiety produces a feeling of resentment, self-conscious resentment and hostility towards the world with which we find ourselves in conflict. We are suddenly aware of our separateness from this world and we experience the pangs of loneliness, of insecurity in our relations with other men. We dread the risk of not belonging, of estrangement from our fellow-man. Our failures give rise to a sense of inferiority, to a sense of guilt, and presently we develop a feeling of doubt about the meaning of our existence, which seems to have no value. To mitigate this feeling of doubt, we develop the habit of self-deception (Sartre's *mauvaise-foi*) in order to conceal from ourselves the painful consciousness of our tragic situation. When we have reached this point in our existential evolution, it is not difficult to persuade us that human life is absurd. Here we are, the only entity in the whole universe with the power of thought, in the midst of inanimate objects and living creatures without intellect, with which we cannot communicate in any way; even with our own fellow humans our means of communication are quite unsatisfactory and often wholly inadequate. Let it be noted here that on this factor of the absurdity of man's situation in the universe there is almost unanimous agreement among all existentialist thinkers.

It is with these and many other corroding and tormenting experiences that oppress us in our daily existence that Existentialism is principally concerned. Who can doubt that the resentfully self-conscious Underground Man was himself the end product of forty years — as he so frequently reminds us — of just such soul-searing experiences? Do you think that the picture of life which the Existentialist draws is too somber, too dismal and too far out of focus with reality? Does this Underground Man exaggerate grossly the darker side of life and exclude the occasional, sometimes even frequent flashes of sunlight? Dostoevsky made him confess as much and made him admit that he had "carried to an extreme" what others "have not dared to carry half way from fear and cowardice to face up to the facts of existence." Apologizing for having committed his evil memories to writing, he tells us: "All the traits for an anti-hero are expressly gathered together here." In creating the Underground Man, Dostoevsky had indeed invented a completely new kind of anti-hero. This personage is of a species wholly different from the anti-heroic *pícaro,* who flourished in Renaissance letters as the antithesis of the perfect gentleman. The Underground Man is the antithesis of the normal, well-balanced man, he is the archetype of the neurotic, resentful, self-pitying, self-deceiving existentialist anti-hero, whose literary fortunes have flourished so brilliantly during the past half-century. Even the literary formula of *Notes from the Underground,* the interrupted monologue, was adopted by Sartre in *La Nausée* and by Camus in *La Chute.*

It is important to observe that the *Notes* is the unique example among Dostoevsky's major works in its consistently *secular* analysis of the human situation. Not once does it raise a religious issue; the Deity is not mentioned nor any symbol of Christian dogma. In this respect, it ranks as Dostoevsky's most sustained flight into pure philosophy, and it may well rank also as the most successful use of the literary art as a medium for philosophical disquisition. Yet in spite of the unique character of this amazing work it is still pure Dostoevsky, both in style and substance. The core idea of each of the two parts of the work is that "our personality, our individuality, is the most precious thing for mankind," freedom of choice is absolutely sacred. But with characteristic perversity, Dostoevsky annihilates his entire argument in the Epilogue, when the Underground Man contradicts himself by saying, "Come now, try to give any one of us... a little more independence, untie our hands, widen the spheres of our activity, relax the control and... we should be begging to be under control again at once." It is hardly necessary to point out that this sudden reversal from free will to determinism is prophetic of the direction of Dostoevsky's future thinking.[2] It anticipates the philosophy of the Grand Inquisitor, which represents Dostoevsky's final analysis of the free will problem; at the same time, it raises this issue to the plane of religious controversy.

Now it is undoubtedly the purely secular, non-religious quality of the *Notes from the Underground* that explains the extraordinary favor this work has enjoyed among the atheistic exponents of Existentialism. These latter have shown far less enthusiasm for Dostoevsky's other major works — *The Idiot, The Possessed,* even for *Crime and Punishment* or *The Brothers Karamazov.* For with *Crime and Punishment* (1866), Dostoevsky began to manifest his pronounced bias in favor of the frame of reference of traditional Christian doctrine, interpreted in his own

---

2. See below, p. 61.

highly individual manner. This does not mean that he renounced by one jot or tittle his views of man's secular nature as these views are expressed in his earlier works — not at all! It means rather that he added to his previous concern with man's existential situation a new and vital concern with man's redemption from his evil nature through the mystical power of Christian love and religious faith. This highly significant broadening of the area of his thinking marks the passage of Dostoevsky from secular to Christian Existentialism. It marks also the beginning of his literary warfare against atheism in general and specifically, against the atheistic materialism of the Russian anarchists led by Bakunin, and the Russian socialists led by Chernishevsky.

The enthusiastic reception accorded to secular Existentialist ideas during the past fifty years outside the Communist orbit can be attributed to the sorry spectacle twentieth century humanity has made of itself in the moral and political fields. While civilized man has pursued his own self-destruction through infinitely ingenious scientific devices, his boasted political sagacity has proved to be totally incompetent to discover the machinery for preventing the holocaust of two world wars. Stifled in an intellectual climate of despair and no longer believing the utopian promises of ameliorative philosophy, the disillusioned intellectuals of Western Europe reacted by turning to the pessimistic realism of Existentialist analysis. Its theoretical fallacies could be disregarded since it fulfilled the very human need for some kind of congenial dialectic to describe *la condition humaine.* The Existentialist vogue got under way in the twenties in Germany, sulking from defeat in World War I. It passed over to France in the thirties, during the barbarous decade of Hitlerian horrors and Stalinian purges. It nourished French intellectuals in World War II.

The present wide diffusion of Existentialist ideas with an atheistic slant among the informed public has been accomplished largely through the medium of the skillful literary presentation of these concepts by Sartre and other French exponents since the last World War. As a result of their fertile literary talent, it is atheistic Existentialism that has predominated during the past half-century. But Existentialism without God is actually a relatively recent and truncated adaptation of a tradition that emerged very early in the writings of Christian theologians. Was it not Tertullian who justified his Christian faith to his pagan Roman opponents with the declaration: "Credo quia absurdum?"[3]

Although the lay public is hardly aware of its vital role in contemporary religious exegesis, this venerable Existentialist tradition in Christian thinking is very much alive today. In its modern aspects it stems from the writings of the non-conformist Danish Lutheran theologian, Sören Kierkegaard, who died in 1855 at the age of 42 years, totally unknown beyond the narrow circle of his theological enemies in Denmark. It was the famous Danish literary historian, Georg Brandes who, in 1900, revealed to

3. This idea was given more elaborate development by St. Anselm (1033-1100), archbishop of Canterbury: "neque enim quaero intellegere ut credam, sed credo ut intellegam."

the Western World the significance of Kierkegaard's highly original religious ideas, which have since proved capable of revitalizing Christian religious philosophy. After a half-century of nearly complete oblivion, Kierkegaard's passionate revolt against the proud, entrenched traditions of official theology became the point of departure for a searching reevaluation of the fundamental bases of Christian doctrine — Catholic, Protestant and Orthodox.

The concerns of secular Existentialist analysis which we have already mentioned — anxiety, estrangement, resentment, loneliness, feelings of guilt, doubt, hypocritical self-deception — all the emotional attributes of the human predicament, with certain qualifications, are included in the Christian existential analysis. However, to these attributes common to both branches of Existentialism, the Christian Existentialist adds certain specifically religious components that distinguish his thinking unmistakably from that of the secular Existentialist.

First, of course, among these religious components is the basic assumption of the existence of God as Creator and Supreme Being, as the Infinite and Eternal. Man is God's creation, God's creature; he properly belongs to God, but he is estranged from God in fact by the corruption of Original Sin, and sin destroys this belonging-to-God relationship. This belief is basic to Christian dogma. Practically, it predicates for man a dual nature — torn internally between good and evil forces, man is in the absurd position of being his own judge, with the knowledge that his judgments will be executed against himself. His every choice involves the possibility of error or sin, and in this sense freedom to choose or free will becomes the principal source of man's anxiety. When we sin, we condemn ourselves and desire punishment for our guilt. We obtain a measure of redemption through confession, and salvation through suffering. Salvation for the Christian Existentialist has been defined as "the act in which the cleavage between man's essential being and his existential predicament is overcome."[4] Yet the lucidity of man's mind constantly reiterates the conscious knowledge that he can never throw off his existential predicament, from which, as Sartre has demonstrated dramatically, there can be *No Exit* (1944).

From this apparent impasse, which leads us very near to despair, the Christian Existentialist does nevertheless find an exit adequate, at least, to save the appearances. To escape from total despair, man must learn first of all to accept himself for what he is — a finite creature, struggling courageously for that faith in divine love which alone can lift the human spirit beyond the meaningless transitoriness of mere existence to the meaningful and purposive contemplation of ultimate redemption. Thus the Christian existential analysis affords at least a ray of hope — not a facile optimism, surely, but sufficient to incite the sincere believer to shape his will to act in accordance with the directives supplied to him by the promptings of religious symbolism, which fulfills man's need for the dramatic confirmation of his faith.

---

4. *Cf.* Paul Tillich, "Existential Analyses and Religious Symbols," in *Contemporary Problems in Religion,* ed. H.A. Basilius, Wayne University Press, 1956; p. 289.

Dostoevsky emerged in 1859 from his ten silent years of exile in Siberia, with his faith in Christian doctrine — which, incidentally, he had never renounced — greatly strengthened after his long and harrowing ordeal. Seven more years elapsed — frustrating years of fruitless effort to achieve financial independence — before he found the suitable occasion to express in literary form his intense religious convictions. Evidence of his growing opposition to the spread of nihilism and materialistic ideas among the new generation of the sixties is recorded in his note-books and diaries of this period. From his published correspondence, we know that he had originally inserted in Chapter Ten, part 2 of the *Notes from the Underground* a passage proclaiming the necessity of religious faith and adjuring meditation upon the Christian mysteries. But this passage was rejected by the official censors and has never been recovered. Thus, it is to *Crime and Punishment* (1866) that we must turn to find the earliest example of Dostoevsky's use of religious elements as an integrated part of a plot. Here, indeed, the resolution of the plot depends wholly and finally upon the slow but certain conversion of Raskolnikov under the guidance of Sonia, the instrument of his ultimate salvation.[5]

His crime, carefully planned and long premeditated, is the result of his loathful resentment against his *condition*

5. This "happy ending" is a re-write; the original *dénouement* depicted the suicide of Raskolnikov — the wages of sin is death. Dostoevsky's editor requested a happy resolution, and obligingly Dostoevsky rewrote the epilogue in keeping with the Christian doctrine of salvation through repentance.

humaine, especially against his own insignificance. To free himself from the lot of an ordinary mortal anything is permitted, and Raskolnikov employs his lucid intelligence relentlessly to establish a logical, rational justification for his evil act. But the crime escapes from the control of his reason — reality is so seldom rational — and once out of control, it assumes a dynamism of its own, unanticipated by its human agent. In working out the design of his crime Raskolnikov has not considered absolutely every contingency — his mind is focused upon his vision of the hated old pawn-broker lying dead on the floor while he ransacks her room for the money that is to save his self-esteem. But the sudden appearance, so unsuspected, of the old pawn-broker's sister impels him to commit a second murder, and it is this rash, impulsive and unplanned crime that staggers him and brings about the rapid dissolution of his personality. Having committed this double murder, Raskolnikov becomes a man of the Underground — a perfect image of the secular Existentialist type — anxious, estranged, hostile, lonely, insecure, guilt-ridden and self-deceiving.

In this instance, however, Dostoevsky granted a brighter future to his anti-hero. His mental anguish and the humiliation of his excessive pride are a proper preparation for Raskolnikov's submission to Christian humility and love. And this love will be embodied in the person of one who has also endured shame and sorrow, Sonia Marmeladov, the regenerated prostitute, the social outcast, who has never lost her simple instinctive faith in Christian redemption. Thus *Crime and Punishment* ends in a positive vein, on a mildly optimistic note of Christian Existentialism. In point of fact, this magnificent novel is an extended parable of salvation through suffering and confession of sin.

In Raskolnikov, Dostoevsky depicted a sinner in search of a soul. By contrast, Prince Myshkin, the protagonist of *The Idiot* (1868), represents the tragedy of the good man in an evil world. Myshkin has spent several years as a mental patient in a Swiss sanatorium. Presumably cured, he returns to St. Petersburg penniless to seek a job that will support his simplest physical needs. Quite by accident, this meek and compassionate prince falls into an environment peopled with unscrupulous bureaucrats, impoverished generals in semi-retirement, grovelling government clerks and, in the offing, a bevy of eligible daughters, restrained by their parents from more than respectable attentions to the prince, whose inheritance has suddenly made him a most desirable catch.

Among these passionately intriguing and wholly unprincipled characters the Prince is admired as a model of goodness, but his influence for good is nil. In this complex and ambiguous novel it is the secondary characters who live out their lives in existential anxiety, resentment and self-deception. Significantly and emphatically Existentialist is the proud and passionate Nastasia Philipovna, torn between the lustful love pressed upon her by the rich and violent Rogozhin and her admiration for the naive and saintly prince, in whose company she finds release from her anguished sense of guilt as the mistress of an old roué. Ashamed of her sinful existence, Nastasia hopes to redeem herself by marrying Myshkin, whose spiritual nobility is recognized by all. But Myshkin proves totally ineffectual with his passive and irresolute temperament he is no match for the wickedly motivated men and women around him, who admire him grudgingly while nicknaming him "the idiot."

Myshkin is weak enough to drop his projected marriage with Aglaya, whom he loves, in order to save Nastasia who fascinates him as a demonic woman to be pitied and redeemed. But Nastasia's awareness of Myshkin's attachment for Aglaya preys upon her mind. As she arrives at the church to be married to Myshkin she catches sight of Rogozhin, rushes to his arms and begs him to take her away with him. When the stupefied prince discovers their whereabouts, Rogozhin shows him the body of Nastasia on the bed where he had killed her upon learning that she did not love him. Nastasia has sacrificed her life in order to free Myshkin to attain his happiness with Aglaya. But the prince decides that he is quite as guilty as Rogozhin, and the novel ends with the rival lovers bedding themselves down together beside the bed of the murdered woman to await their arrest. When questioned by the police, Myshkin cannot answer, he has lost his reason completely. He has become in very fact the "idiot" that he had so long been nicknamed.

In *The Idiot* Dostoevsky used for the first time a myth of which he was especially fond — the myth of the descent of Christ to the Earth, the same legend he employed later so much more effectively in the "Legend of the Grand Inquisitor" found in his last novel, *The Brothers Kara-mazov* (1880). Derived as it is from this venerable Christian legend, the enigma of Myshkin's character can

best be explained in terms of Christian Existentialist
analysis. Dostoevsky first conceived the Prince as the
Christ-like embodiment of a spirit that had taken on the
flesh of humanity, without its evil passions. To his
companions, Myshkin appears as a positively good man;
yet in their estimation, his conduct is altogether absurd.
Thus arose the paradox that tortured the artistic sense of
our author; how could he reconcile within a single fictional
hero the absurd with the good in such a way as to produce
a character spiritually credible and at the same time
recognizably and convincingly human? According to
Dostoevsky himself, his idea of Myshkin's character
originated in his special fondness for the lovable Spanish
knight-errant, Don Quixote, and there is surely much that
is quixotic in Myshkin's actions. But the comparison of
Cervantes' hero with Myshkin cannot be successfully
pressed very far. Myshkin's absurdities are never funny, he
never makes us laugh with those sallies of wit and wisdom
that make us love the mad Spanish knight. In short,
Myshkin is unable to make us love him as a person or to
accept his eccentric behavior as authentic. No, Dostoevsky
did not quite succeed in his attempt to present in positive
form (as he said) a really good man. What he did
accomplish brilliantly in *The Idiot* was rather the dramatic
depiction of the enormous contrast between the Christian
ideal and the existential life of a representative section of
the Russian people in the middle of the last century, and
also, in the character of Nastasia, a very nearly complete
and perfect image of a heroic woman as conceived in terms
of Christian Existentialism. The sensationally macabre and

melodramatic ending is a rather shoddy device to conceal
the author's quandary regarding the proper and further
destiny of his hero. The very Christian prince Myshkin is
quite definitely a negative exhibit in the Christian Existentialist gallery. At the conclusion of the novel, it is clear
that Dostoevsky had reached the conviction that the role
of the good man in an evil world is artistically incommen-
surable with the conception of a victory of virtue over
vice.

In proportion as the political climate of the 1860's
became more tense and terroristic activities gathered
momentum in every corner of European Russia, Dostoevsky grew more and more vehemently outspoken in
opposition to every aspect of liberal thought. Already in
The Idiot he voiced his hatred of liberalism in no uncertain
terms:

> "I have discovered that Russian liberalism is not an
> attack on the existing order of things, but an attack on
> the very essence of things, on the things themselves,
> and not only on their order, not on the Russian system
> of government, but on Russia herself; my liberal has
> gone so far as to deny Russia herself; that is to say he
> hates and beats his own mother... He hates national
> customs, he hates Russian history, he hates every-
> thing."

With the publication in 1872 of the stormy and strident
novel *The Possessed* (or *The Devils*), Dostoevsky accomplished his long-cherished design of dealing a body blow to

the hated liberals. *The Possessed* is a savage and belligerent assault upon science, reason, revolution, socialists, atheists, the Roman Church, the aristocracy, Westernizers (especially Turgenev), political reforms, terrorists, nihilists — in a word, against everything which the author had grown to hate as his opinions hardened into violent prejudices. What Dostoevsky wished to propose in place of modernism is perhaps best expressed, in this novel, by Shatov, the ill-starred renegade from the terrorist group, who pays with his life the penalty exacted by his former associates for breaking with them and their nihilistic activities. It is the reformed Shatov who declares:

> "The purpose of the whole evolution of a nation, in every people and at every period of its existence is solely the pursuit of God, and faith in Him as in the only true one. God is the synthetic personality of the whole people.... A truly great people can never reconcile itself to playing second fiddle in the affairs of humanity.... Only one nation among all the nations can have the true God... and the only God-fearing people is the Russian people."

This confession of faith, which is, of course, Dostoevsky's own personal confession, ends with the much-quoted passage: "I believe in Russia. I believe in the Greek Orthodox Church. I believe in the body of Christ. I believe that the second coming will take place in Russia." "But do you believe in God?" Stavrogin asks him, and Shatov haltingly replies: "I--I shall believe in God."

This enigmatic future tense — "I shall believe..." — has elicited a wide variety of critical interpretations, from the completely liberal to the transcendentally metaphysical. I should like to suggest that Dostoevsky, who through the medium of pen and ink poured out the very distillation of himself — his greatness and his pettiness, his noble ideas along with his irrational notions — Dostoevsky reveals in this famous future tense the ultimate uncertainty of his will-to-believe; he is clinging instinctively and desperately to the immeasurably comforting hope of a future revelation of God's existence. We may solve this troublesome enigma, I think, simply by regarding it as a paradoxical expression quite characteristic of Christian existential analysis.

There are, of course, numerous examples of secular Existentialist types in this sprawling, dynamic novel. There is, for instance, Stavrogin, lucid of mind but morally a mass of contradictions, guilt-ridden, destined for suicide; there are the two Verkhovensky's, the father, Stephen, representative of the generation of the liberals, the "superfluous men" of the forties, whose son Peter has become the organizer of the terrorists of the sixties, and incidentally, one of the blackest scoundrels in all literature; and there is Kirillov, prepared to shoot himself at any time to prove the terrible freedom of his own self-will and the non-existence of God. Yet it is the Christian element that triumphs in the end, when old Verkhovensky throws off his former free-thinking conventions on his death bed and declares:

"J'ai menti toute ma vie... The whole law of human existence consists merely of making it possible for every man to bow down before what is infinitely great. If man were to be deprived of the infinitely great, he would refuse to go on living, and die in despair. The infinite and the immeasurable are as necessary to man as the little planet he inhabits... Long live the great idea! The eternal, the immeasurable Great Idea!"

Lest we forget that our author's immediate and impelling purpose in writing *The Possessed* was to exorcise the curse of nihilism and terrorism which had crazed the youth of Russia and turned them into devils, Dostoevsky assures us that this danger will finally pass away, and he finds justification for his optimism in the parable of the Gadarene swine, as told in the Gospel of St. Luke (8: 32-36):

"All the impurities, all the big and little devils that have accumulated in our great and beloved invalid, in our Russia, for centuries ... all those devils, all those abominations will themselves ask to enter into swine ... and we shall cast ourselves down, we the raving and possessed, from the cliff into the sea and shall all be drowned; and serves us right, for that is all we are good for. But the sick man Russia will be healed and will sit at the feet of Jesus, and all will look upon him and be amazed."

What an effective use of religious symbolism to confirm the Existentialist faith — the Christian Existentialist faith — in salvation through confession and suffering! Even old Verkhovensky feels he has achieved redemption, but there remains in his mind a lingering doubt. He will not assert his salvation as a certain knowledge, he merely asks the question: "If I have come to love God and rejoice in my love, is it possible that he should extinguish both me and my joy and turn us into nothingness? If God exists, then I, too, am immortal!"

Of all Dostoevsky's works, *The Possessed* remains most contemporaneous to our troubled times. Reading this novel today, with the hindsight afforded by the Communist Revolution in Russia, we are sure to be struck by the prophetic insights of the author. Not only did he foretell the type of persons who would emerge as leaders of the Communist Party, but he also revealed the organizational structure which the Communists were to use so effectively to defy the harshest police measures which the czarist government could devise for their suppression. This was, of course, based upon the party cell with its members sworn to absolute secrecy and blind obedience to their unitary leader.

Dostoevsky documented with careful investigation his satirical depiction of this ingenious organizational device of the Russian terrorists of the 1860's and '70's. Although living abroad during the history-making months of L'Affaire Netchaev,[6] he was able to follow the accounts of

---

6. Sergey Netchaev (1847-1882), conspirator for revolution, agitator for student uprising of 1868-69; he "talked up" student violence in St. Petersburg, published two issues of *Popular Violence* in Switzerland. He was extradited as a criminal to Russia in 1872, and spent the last ten years of his life imprisoned in St. Peter's and St. Paul's prison fortress.

the student riots in the journals available to him. These hectic days are recorded and incorporated in his *Note-Books for the Possessed.* After a strenuous purging of the brute facts of these events, Dostoevsky introduced in the pages of *The Possessed* recognizable elements of this forerunner of far greater uprisings in the Russian capital. There is no doubt that Netchaev served as a greatly modified model for the villainous Peter Verkhovensky, who seeks to wreak his criminal designs against all who challenge his leadership of his cell.

Publication of *The Possessed* (1871-1872) won for Dostoevsky the lasting friendship of the powerful official Procurator of the Holy Synod, Konstantine Pobedonost-sev, influential in affairs of both Church and State. Their meeting of minds led to Dostoevsky's acceptance of the editorship of *The Citizen,* a weekly publication sponsored by Prince Metchersky as an organ of conservative thought. For *The Citizen,*[7] Dostoevsky wrote several journalese articles revealing his own political thinking as well as a half-dozen short stories — "Vlas," "The Queer Fellow" and that masterpiece of the macabre genre, "Bobok."[8] However, for understanding the conservative cast of the editor's thinking, it is his political articles that are of prime importance; here we find the veritable expression of the

7. Most of D's. contributions to *The Citizen* are included in the excellently Englished edition by Boris Brasol, *Diary of a Writer,* New York, Scribner; 2 vols., 1949.

8. Ed. Brasol, v. I, "Vlas," pp. 31-42; "Bobok," pp. 43-57; "The Queer Fellow," English title, "The Dream of a Queer Fellow,"" *ibidem,* pp. 490-527; published in English translation, London, Unwin, 1916 (several reprints).

ripe years of his conservatism that defies the myth-making interpretation of contemporary critics that would transport this very thoughtful conservative into the camp of the liberal collectivist ranks.[9] An example of Dostoevsky's political thinking is found in the last issue of *The Citizen* (March, 1874);[10] here he takes exception to the annual report of the Minister of Public Instruction, wherein this official stated, "after the inspection of the educational institutions he could report that 'in recent years our youth has adopted an infinitely more serious attitude toward the problem of learning and has been studying far more diligently.' "

Dostoevsky interprets this to imply that the fomentors of student uprisings and violent confrontations incited by Netchaev are found only among the idle defectives and not at all among youths attending to their studies. "What if it should happen," asks Dostoevsky, "that the diligent, enthusiastic youths attending precisely to their studies, should be endowed with good but only misdirected hearts?" And he proceeds to remind his readers that

---

9. Professor Simon Karlinsky, "Dostoevsky as Rorschach Test," *N.Y. Times Book Review*, June 13, 1971, reviews in lead article the critical estimates of Dostoevsky's writings succinctly but justly over the past eighty years, to show the enormity of the misrepresentation and distortion of the novelist's ideas in order "to construct their own systems of supposedly Dostoyevskian thought (often unwarranted by the texts of the novels or the known views of the novelist) and ... bend the knee before their own creations in worshipful wonder."

10. This extraordinarily self-revealing article is entitled "One of the Contemporaneous Falsehoods," Brasol, *op. cit.*, I, pp. 142-154.

"There are swindlers who are very crafty and who have studied precisely the magnanimous phase of the human — usually youthful — soul, so as to be able to play on it as on a musical instrument." At this point, Dostoevsky tells his readers that he knew from personal experience that activist youths are not necessarily recruited from among mere idlers who have learned nothing. "I am an old activist myself. I stood on the scaffold condemned to death, and I assure you that I stood there in the company of educated people; some of them had graduated from the highest institutions of learning; some distinguished themselves later by remarkable works in special fields. No, Netchaevtsí are not always recruited from among idlers who learn nothing... Probably I could never have become a Netchaev, but a Netchaevétz — for this I wouldn't vouch; maybe I could have become one in the days of my youth; our group was contaminated with the ideas of the then prevailing theoretical socialism."

§

Since the invasion of Western civilization by the revolutionary social doctrines of Marx, of Bakunin, along with the propaganda of dozens of other prophets of collectivist-oriented panaceas, the works of Dostoevsky have been subjected to a strange and startling interpretation. They are acclaimed as adjuncts of revolutionary doctrines; they are hailed as food for advanced revolutionary tastes and have been buried beneath a protective coating of sociological profundity of unequaled more-than-meets-the-eye implications. In France, for example, Sartre and Camus claimed Dostoevsky as a greatly misunderstood liberal, who wrote about the Russian common people, loved them and understood them and suffered deeply because of their plight in a world totally unconcerned with their physical and moral needs. In the last issue of *The Citizen* (March, 1874), Dostoevsky explained briefly the three kinds of governments: "Oligarchs are thinking only about the interests of the rich; democracy is thinking only about the interests of the poor — but the commonweal, the good of all the people, is at present nobody's concern, save that of socialistic dreamers and positivists boosting science and expecting everything from it — a new communion of men and new principles on which the social organism should be founded — for once, mathematically secure and immovable principles. However, science from which so much is expected, is hardly in a position to tackle this problem forthwith.... . To the millions of the demos, save for all too rare exceptions, the plunder of property-owners is the principal object, the crown of all desires." This comment upon the pretensions of the masses represents his true and steadfast political stand on the socio-economic dialogue during his mature years.

Recently, Professor Karlinsky has discussed the widespread habit among *littérateurs* and commentators to draw upon Dostoevsky's novels to lend an air of finality to their analysis of a wide variety of human activities — crime, sex, theological strictures, psychiatry, sociological nostrums and what-have-you.[11] Karlinsky reminds these would-be

---

11. *Cf.* note 9 above.

seekers of truth in Dostoevsky's novels that this great
writer of novels was not a philosopher, but an observer,
among the very greatest, "of the human condition, who
measured the depths of man's quivering heart with all its
struggles, sins and tempests, its unseen tears and burning
passions." Although Dostoevsky was well-read in philosophical writings, he was not attracted to experiment at
length with abstract thinking. His fictional creations are
the concretization of his abstract concepts, vitalized,
animated with contradictory desires and existential
options.

Unquestionably, Dostoevsky was proud of his achievements as a novelist and was happiest when working on the
plan and characters of a new enterprise in fiction. This
explains his resignation (1874) as editor of *The Citizen*,[12]
a well-paid position, to write *A Raw Youth* (1875), his
least successful novel. Arkady Dolgoruky is a young fellow
bent on social climbing through the acquisition of money,
which provides the power over men and things that this
uninteresting hero desires. The author tries to arouse the
reader's interest by several extended episodes revealing the
rebuffs and the victories experienced by Arkady, ending
with a belated realization that "all that glitters is not
gold." Financially, this new novel sold well for a brief
period; on the whole, however, it was a disappointment to
both author and public.[13]

---

12. D. retained managerial functions of editor through most of the
month of April, 1875.

13. His two novels, *The Gambler* (1866) and *The Eternal Husband*
(1870) were potboilers; briefly successful in Russia, they are rated
critically as notably inferior to the five masterpieces with which we
are here concerned.

Dostoevsky soon decided to try his hand both as author and promoter of *The Diary of a Writer,* to be issued monthly beginning in January, 1876. Successful beyond the fondest hopes of the founder-author, 13,000 subscriptions were bought by a highly satisfied public. But again, the novelist rebelled against the journalist; Dostoevsky announced that the last number of *The Diary* would appear at the end of the year 1877. His mind was already preoccupied with the formulation of the story line and establishing the conflicting roles of *The Brothers Karamazov,* the last and surely the greatest of his novels. It would begin to appear serially in *The Russian Messenger* for January, 1879; it was issued in book form in the spring of 1880. It is to this work we wish now to turn.

•

Reflections on "The Grand Inquisitor"

IN THE SPRING and summer months of 1879, in his fifty-eighth year, Feodor Michailovitch Dostoevsky completed the final version of the fifth of the twelve sections of *The Brothers Karamazov,* under the section-heading "Pro et Contra." On the 10th of May, he sent off the final draft of the first four chapters of this section, to *The Russian Messenger* in Moscow, for publication in the June issue of that review. To explain his failure to include the three remaining chapters of the section, he enclosed with his manuscript a covering-letter, addressed to the assistant editor Liubimov, disclosing his own evaluation of the critical importance of the fifth chapter entitled "The Grand Inquisitor" that he was still working on. Without doubt, this famous chapter contains the most philosophic and the most controversial of all Dostoevsky's voluminous writings. That he was well aware of the high significance of this lengthy chapter Dostoevsky made clear in the most crucial paragraph of his note to Liubimov:

"This is the Fifth Book, entitled 'Pro et Contra'.... In my view, this Fifth Book is the culminating point of the whole novel, and it must be executed with special care. The idea of it is to depict the extreme blasphemy and the core of the destructive ideas of our present age in Russia among the young people who are divorced from reality ... and along with the blasphemy and anarchism, the refutation of them, which I am now preparing in the second part of this section in the dying words of Father Zossima. In the manuscript I have just sent off, I have simply depicted the character of one of the principal personages of the novel, who is expressing his fundamental convictions. I regard these convictions as a synthesis of contemporary Russian anarchism — denial not of God, but of the meaning of his creation.... . My hero states a thesis which is, in my opinion, irresistible — the senselessness of the suffering of children — from which he deduces the absurdity of all historical reality. I don't know whether I have done this well, but I do know that my hero Ivan is in the highest degree real. His blasphemy will be triumphantly refuted in the next release."[14]

Whether or not Dostoevsky succeeded in refuting Ivan's blasphemy as he promised to do in the "next release" is a moot question. Ivan's refusal to accept the sufferings of innocent children as consistent with a universal order controlled by an omnipotent Creator will seem justifiable to rationally-minded readers as a logical and credible

14. Constantine Mochulski reproduces this letter in full in his excellent literary biography, *Dostoïevski: l'homme et l'oeuvre*, Paris, Payot, 1963; p. 490-91.

deduction. To excuse this horror, we should have to accept the controversial Pauline-Augustinian thesis of "universal original sin," of which the inevitable "wages is death" — haphazardly, sooner or later.

No one will take issue, however, with the author's claim that his hero is "in every sense real." That this is true is attested by Dostoevsky's repeated admissions in his correspondence regarding his own religious doubts. For example, he wrote of himself in 1854: "I am a child of the present age; a child of disbelief and doubts up to this time, and even — I surely know it — up to the very grave."[15] Ivan's doubts are surely the very same doubts that the younger Dostoevsky had experienced in his own earlier years. These doubts he could recount in harsh, realistically dramatic fashion with the deepest conviction, from his own personal knowledge of the mental torture, the emotional excitement of the agnostic dialectic. His most recent important biographer, Mochul'ski, ascribes the revolt of Ivan Karamazov against Christian doctrine directly to the author's deep personal sorrow at the death (1868) of his first-born child Sonia, at the age of only three months: "Dostoevsky had seen his daughter's face, unique, irreplaceable, eternal, unforgettable. This revelation of personality posed with stupefying force the crucial question of personal resurrection, which is really the subject of *The Brothers Karamazov.* Soon after Sonia's death, Dostoevsky wrote: 'Where is that little personality, for whose life I would have undergone gladly the death on

---

15. *Cf.* Vladimir Seduro, *Dostoevski in Russian Literary Criticism, 1846-1956,* New York, Columbia University Press, 1957; p. 24-42.

the cross?"[16] Dostoevsky perpetuated the memory of his youngest son, who died in 1878 at the very time the author was beginning work on his great novel, by giving his dead son's name Alyosha to the third brother, who chose the priesthood as his calling.

Dostoevsky's judgment of the importance, the seriousness of "The Legend of the Grand Inquisitor" was entirely correct; certainly, it is not a flippant exercise of the author's romantic imagination.[17] Not only does it stand as the culminating point of his most impressive novel, but it is generally regarded as the supreme example of literary irony in all world literature. The complex significance of this profound and moving indictment of human nature and (by inference) of the Christian Church — not, it must be stressed, of the Christian religion — has challenged the searching analysis of scores of able though often wrong-headed critics. Quite rightly, they have sought to wring every drop of meaning from this masterpiece.

Here we propose to discuss briefly three very modest but challenging facets of the famous chapter, facets that

16. *Cf.* Mochulski, *op. cit.*, p. 276.

17. The most probable prototype of Dostoevsky's grand inquisitor is the unsavory personage in Schiller's *Don Carlos,* who appears in the last scene of the play (Act V, scene 8) to receive from the king's hands his only son and heir for immolation. "Don Carlos honors mankind? How then can he be fit to be king?" Dostoevsky greatly admired this play and read it through many times. Yet, what a gulf separates the two inquisitors! Schiller's remains a shadowy, secondary character, Dostoevsky's an overpowering figure, the monstrous impersonation of tyranny incarnate. *Cf.* Robert Payne, *Dostoevsky: a Human Portrait,* New York, Knopf, 1961; p. 358-59.

we believe deserve thoughtful consideration. First, the question is often raised: why did the deeply religious Dostoevsky make such an ungracious and unkind attack upon the Roman Church, representing that ancient and honorable institution in such unfavorable posture as he seems to have done in "The Grand Inquisitor?" The too obvious answer to this problem is that Dostoevsky, being of the Eastern Orthodox persuasion, would hardly choose to condemn so categorically and completely his own particular and personal religion. How can we explain in depth this savage attack upon the Roman Church?[18]

Dostoevsky's assault is clearly aimed at the Roman institution, but surely this is not his ultimate goal. Through the most distinguished and the most powerful of the Western religious bodies he is striking indirectly, with his most astringent ironies, at the basic cultural dogmas of Western civilization. He is challenging what he held to be a fundamental, schizophrenic hypocrisy in Western culture — namely, the doctrine of the double truth — the truth of Faith and the truth of Natural Reason[19] — what the German theologians call "Das Prinzip der doppelten

18. Dostoevsky had previously attacked the Roman Church directly in *The Idiot* (1869): "It is an unchristian religion in the first place. It is worse than atheism, it preaches a distorted Christ. Roman Catholicism believes the Church cannot exist on earth without universal temporal power; they have added lies, fraud, deceit, fanaticism, superstition, wickedness. They have trifled with the most sacred, truthful innocent ardent feelings of the people; they have bartered it all for money, for base temporal power." (Magarshak's translation, Penguin Classics edition, p. 585-86.)

19. All quotations from the text of "The Grand Inquisitor" are from Magarshak's translation cited above, n. 1.

Wirchlichkeit." It is the 80-year old Cardinal — the Grand
Inquisitor himself — who reveals this fact to the reader,
when he says to Christ:

> "Peacefully the people will die, peacefully they will
> pass away in your name, and beyond the grave they
> will find nothing but death. But we shall keep this
> *secret* for ourselves, and for their happiness we will
> entice them with the reward of heaven and eternity.
> For even if there were anything at all in the next world,
> it would not be for such as they. They believe and
> predict that you will come again victoriously, to rule
> the world perfected; we shall tell them that they have
> indeed saved themselves by their good obedience to our
> doctrines. Actually, of course, it is we who have saved
> them, all of them — by saving them from their
> freedom, from rebellion; for they have resigned their
> freedom to us and have submitted their lives unto our
> charge."

This is rather strong language — and indeed, it is the
most sweeping criticism anywhere in literature against the
doctrine of free-will, and also against the doctrine of
reconciliation of faith and reason. Moreover, it is without
doubt an ironic summary of Dostoevsky's bitter and
self-righteous anger with the West. It betokens the deep
psychological gulf between Russian and Western religious
sensibilities.

During the Middle Ages, while the Roman Church was
busily organizing itself under a single bishop, the Bishop of

Rome, the Eastern patriarchs were obstinately refusing to unite their forces against the hordes of Mohammedans and Tartars overrunning the entire Eastern Empire — to the ultimate capture of Constantinople itself. Endlessly, Eastern theologians quibbled about such doctrinal enigmas as the question of the single or dual nature of Christ, the so-called Christological controversy. Meanwhile, the West was gradually and dangerously attacking the long and painful process of rationalizing its theology — to reconcile the myths of religion with observed phenomena of mundane existence. Man's curiosity about his environment in physical nature, his awareness of the need to comprehend his situation within the encompassing universe led him to seek outside the strictures of theology for comprehensive secular knowledge of this world and of man's place in it.

For centuries, the class-rooms of the Faculty of Theology in the University of Paris resounded with the disputations of masters and students debating points of doctrine, displaying their skill in dialectic — balancing faith against reason.[20] The result was a dichotomy; theology in

---

20. A famous example of Scholastic dialectic is the extended commentary by Nicole Oresme, written in 1377, in Bk. II, ch. 25, of his French translation and commentary of Aristotle's *De Caelo, Le Livre du Ciel et du Monde* (ed. Menut, Univ. of Wisconsin Press, p. 519-39, fols. 137d-144c); Madison, 1968. In this discussion of a heliocentric versus a geocentric universe, Oresme produces ten arguments in support of the former system — all ten used by Copernicus two and a half centuries later. However, the discussion ends as follows: "... to an eye in the heavens, which could see the earth clearly, the earth would appear to move; if the eye were on the

the West became a house divided, and from this conflict of interests there sprang forth the secular branches of learning. Over the centuries, this rationalized curiosity about the physical world developed into our contemporary natural and exact sciences, introducing controlled and precisely measured experiment. Scientific methodology arose as a result of Western man's compelling need to explain in realistic rational terms the often unrational myths and mysteries of Christian mythology.

This confusing intrusion of science into the realm of theological study and discipline looms large in the history of Western culture. In the history of Eastern Orthodox Christianity, it is almost totally missing. In the East there was no codification of a unitary body of doctrine. There was, rather, the private individual teaching of Christian traditions, striving for saintliness and the power to perform miracles, handing on the customary doctrines from generation to generation, carefully preserved in great detail by word of mouth and by example, uncodified and contained only in the sayings of such saintly men as Sergius of Zhitomir or Vladimir of Rostov or the greatly revered Eighteenth Century monk Tikhon of Zadonsk, whom

---

earth, the heavens would appear to move. It cannot be demonstrated conclusively by argument that the heavens move, and we have offered arguments opposing their diurnal motion. However, everyone thinks, and I myself think, that the heavens do move and not the earth. For God hath established the world which shall not be moved, in spite of contrary reasons, because they are clearly not conclusive persuasions.... What I have said by way of diversion or intellectual exercise can in this manner serve as a valuable means of refuting and checking those who would like to impugn our faith by argument."

Dostoevsky could very well have chosen as his model of the perfect Christian saint in the personage of Father Zossima in *The Brothers Karamazov*.[21]

Thus the Eastern Church is first of all the self-conscious repository and preserver of ritual and ceremony dating from the time of the early Christian communities. It has shunned all traffic with the principle of the double truth; it avoids contamination by secular interests of every sort, seeking to remain the eternally unsullied vessel of Christianity, in which alone is retained the veritable Divine Image of Christ. It remains closest to a pure, unadulterated theological theology among contemporary Christian creeds. The pictorial delineation of the creed is preserved in the ikons that abound in the centuries-old churches and monasteries of every Eastern Orthodox country.

It was to this Eastern Orthodox Church, to its doctrines and its ritualistic devotion to the traditional

---

21. In the spring of 1878, Dostoevsky discussed at length with his friend Pobedonostsev, future procurator-general of the Holy Synod, his wish to acquaint himself with the routine of life for the monks in a Russian Orthodox monastery. Pobedonostsev obliged his petitioner by arranging for Dostoevsky, together with his friend, the philosopher Vladimir Solovyov as companion, to spend a few days at the Optina monastery. The guests arrived on June 18th and were welcomed by Father Ambrosii, the director. They spent four days conversing with the scholarly director and in observing the activities of the monks in the famous hermitage. As a result of this experience, the description of the daily activities of the monks under Father Zossima is attributable to Dostoevsky's observations at the Optina Hermitage, while the thoughts expressed by Father Zossima derive in large part from D's. reading of *The Life and Deeds of the Schismatic Monk Zossima*, published Moscow, 1860. More on Pobedonostsev, below, page 72.

Christian dogmata that Dostoevsky gave his loyal though not uncritical support upon his return from exile in 1859. He had left St. Petersburg for Siberia on Christmas Day, 1849, in his twenty-eighth year, under the all-pervading influence of advanced Western ideas — the utopian, humanitarian socialism of the French Saint-Simoniens, Fouriéristes, Lamennais, the rationalistic, pragmatic Utilitarianism of Bentham and Ricardo, and the romantic metaphysics of Hegel and Schleiermacher. As one of the first generation of Russian intelligentsia of the 19th century, Dostoevsky was a progressive liberal, a Western-izer and the author of two successful novels of social justice; presaging his later interest in abnormal psychology, he anticipated Stevenson's *Doctor Jekyll and Mr. Hyde* in a novel entitled *The Double.*

Dostoevsky returned to European Russia in 1859, after four years of hard labor in chains and four years of military service as a private in Omsk and Semipalatinsk. His experiences in exile had converted him to the nationalistic doctrine that is broadly defined as Slavo-philism: Russia must work out its own salvation free from Western influences in philosophy, in politics, in technical development — above all, in religion. Briefly, Russia must abandon the fallacious socialistic, humanitarian direction of materialistic, industrialized Western Europe; it must develop its traditional theocratic-political institutions under the guidance of the Orthodox doctrine endorsed by the autocratic control of the czarist government. This conviction was intensified immeasurably by the eight years (1863-71) spent largely in Western Europe, unhappy years that deepened Dostoevsky's conviction that "materialism must certainly lead to universal corruption and the mechanical sciences mean death."

Quite by chance, Dostoevsky's return to literary activity in the early 1860's coincided with a period of exceptional intellectual ferment and social turbulence among Russia's intelligentsia — what we have come to call the Second Russian Enlightenment. The wave of the new science from Western Europe swept through the ranks of young Russian intellectuals at the precise moment when the latter were intoxicated with the euphoria created by the emancipation of the serfs (1863). In the West, Faraday had revolutionized physical science by putting electricity to work; Darwin had dipped into man's remotest past to link his origins irrefutably with the animal kingdom; in Paris, in his exiguous laboratory, Claude Bernard was experimenting boldly with the chemistry of the human body, seeking to discover the secret of the mechanical nature of human activity, mental and physical. One of Bernard's most enthusiastic adherents was the young Russian, Ivan Sechenov (1829-1905), who had studied medicine in Germany and was destined to found behavioristic psychology, to pass on to his world-renowned successor, Ivan Pavlovitch Pavlov, the basic concept of the conditioned reflex which Pavlov verified in his experiments with salivating dogs. Today in Moscow, the Sechenov Institute, built in 1955, stands as a tribute to the memory of the earliest of Russia's numerous contributors to physiological studies.

Dostoevsky nowhere mentions Sechenov by name in his writings, but it is hardly likely that he did not know about Sechenov's famous run-in with the censorship, which forbade publication in 1861 of Sechenov's doctoral dissertation entitled "An Attempt to explain physiologically the origin of psychic phenomena." In 1863 the censor did allow publication of a greatly abbreviated redaction in a medical journal under the title "Brain Reflexes." For eight years Sechenov sought in vain to get his basically physiological approach to human mental activity published in full; meanwhile, the censor's perennial refusal created a perpetual conflict between government and intelligentsia.[22]

Then there were also the technological inventions — steam locomotives that began the annihilation of space, intensified in our own day in the air above us with jets and super-jets; the telegraph spread its network of wires across national boundaries; illuminating gas was piped to palaces and private homes and lighted the streets in cities throughout the continent.

All these new and startling developments in man's interpretation and use of his material world had to be assimilated and adapted by the younger generation of the sixties and seventies. Political theories had to be devised to fit this new image of the world. Inevitably, some of the

22. Although D. was absent from Russia during most of the Sechenov struggle with the censorship, he was in correspondence with persons of conservative views who would naturally inform him of matters relating to the censorship. The history of the case is reviewed briefly in R.F. Byrnes' excellent study, *Pobedonostsev, His Life and Thought*, Indiana University Press, 1968, p. 93-108.

heories proposed were wildly revolutionary. For example, here was Chernishevsky with his proto-Marxian economics of class-war, whom Dostoevsky ridiculed in *The Possessed*; here was Pisarev, the intellectual exponent of Nihilism, with Nechaev acting out in real life the violent destruction of useless persons – Nechaev is permanently installed as the ultimate example of brutal villainy in the personage of Peter Verkhovensky, just as the anarchist Kirillov, also in *The Possessed*, is Dostoevsky's cartoon of the self-exiled arch-anarchist philosophizer Bakunin.

Watching these events from his listening-post in Wiesbaden, Turgenev described unforgettably in *Fathers and Sons* (1862) the transformation of Russia under the impact of the new ideas, without taking sides. It was Turgenev's objectivity that angered Dostoevsky, who turned Turgenev into Karmazinov, the vulgar caricature who consorts with the Nihilists in *The Possessed*. Even the autocratic government of Russia felt the impact of this "wave of the future" and reacted with the Great Reforms of the sixties and seventies, beginning with the emancipation of the serfs (1861), trial by jury (1864), extension of public education (1864), relaxation of censorship (1865), taxation rates fixed at the local level (1870), Army reform (1874).

Of these basic reforms, Dostoevsky approved only the first – the abolition of serfdom. His opposition to trial by jury is dramatically expressed in the miscarriage of justice at the trial of Dmitri Karamazov, who is judged guilty of the killing of his father, the crime actually committed by the illegitimate, epileptic son Smerdyakov, under the false impression that he was acting out the secret sub-conscious wish of his adored half-brother, the agnostic Ivan. Dostoevsky abhorred profoundly the rapid drift toward materialistic secularism, the threatened disappearance of the traditional reverence for religion and the violence of the contest between Holy Russia and the unholy West, which had surrendered to the evil influence of materialistic science — to the scientism in which the only realities were matter and motion. As though recoiling from his own youthful radicalism, he veered toward the established powers, Church and State, as preservers of political stability and public order.

What Dostoevsky is attacking in the "Grand Inquisitor" with all the ironic power of his superior literary artistry is, of course, the rationalistic Utopianism of Western humanitarianism — what we call today Progressive Liberalism, the prevailing optimistic idea that men are somehow capable of establishing a rational, ordered socio-political system in which they retain their essential freedoms — above all, freedom of will to choose their own course of action, and further, that such a system — the open state, we call it — will produce a maximum of human happiness. According to this theory, men are by nature good — as Rousseau insisted. What is needed is a rational code of laws and regulations to direct man's social and political activities, exactly like the laws of motion that govern the movements of physical objects.

For if there are mechanical laws for the inanimate physical world, then by analogy there should be dependable formulae for the management of socio-political behavior. All that is required is the transfer of the methods so successful in the exact sciences to the problems of managing a reasonable and orderly human society. As a famous Dutch scientist has remarked: "The conceptual vista ahead for the 19th century intellectual was optimistically the complete mechanization of the world picture — men and machines operating harmoniously under one and the same general principle."[23] Today, a century later, this idea seems both naïve and preposterous, even repulsive, and this fact is due in no small part to the impressive opposition of Feodor Michailovitch Dostoevsky, the non-organization man par excellence. His quarrel with his contemporaries of liberal persuasion was basically due to his certain knowledge, purely instinctive, that human beings cannot be equated with machines — that they are essentially schizoids, torn between will and reason, with the will always in the ascendant through any extended period of time. This overwhelming force of irrationality in mankind precludes any reasonable or ordered institutionalized society. The social panaceas offered by the social humanitarians — the labor movements, the nihilists, the communists — all these must fail. For, as Ippolit in *The Idiot* declares: "It is life, life that matters — the continuous and everlasting process of discovering it and not the discovery itself";[24] and this acute awareness of the flow of existence, its creative continuity recalls the Underground Man's insistence that "reason knows only what it has

---

23. *Cf.* E.J. Dijksterhuis, *Mechanization of the World Picture*, Oxford, Clarendon, 1961, p. 495.

24. Ed. Magarshak, p. 433.

succeeded in learning, while human nature acts as a whole... and even if it goes wrong, it lives![25][25]

This same emphasis upon man's will to live recurs in *The Brothers Karamazov,* in the discussion between the two brothers — Ivan the agnostic and Alyosha the young priest. Their discussion precedes the chapter entitled "The Grand Inquisitor." Ivan says:

"If I didn't believe in life, if I lost faith in the order of things, if I were convinced that everything was, on the contrary, a disorderly, a damnable and perhaps a devil-ridden chaos, if I were completely overcome by all the horrors of man's disillusionment — I'd still want to live, and having once raised the cup to my lips, I wouldn't tear myself away from it till I had drained it to the dregs! I've asked myself many times, is there in the world any despair that would overcome this frenzied and perhaps indecent thirst for life in me ... Alyosha, I want to live and I go on living, even if it is against logic. I still love the sticky little leaves that open up in the spring, I love the blue sky, I love some people ... without knowing why; I love some great human accomplishment in which I've perhaps lost faith long ago, but which my heart still reveres. I'm going abroad, Alyosha, to Europe, knowing that I'm only going to a graveyard, but it's a most precious graveyard; yes, indeed, precious are the dead that lie there. Every stone over them speaks of such ardent life in the past, of such passionate faith in their achievements, their

25. *Vide supra,* p. 16.

truth, their struggles and their science, that I know beforehand that I shall fall on the ground and kiss those stones and weep over them; but at the same time, I am deeply convinced that Europe has long been a graveyard and nothing more. It is not a matter of intellect or logic. You love it all with your insides, with your belly; you love to feel your youthful powers asserting themselves for the first time."

To this Alyosha replies: "One longs to love with one's insides, with one's belly, and I think everyone must love life more than anything else in the world."

To which the rationalist Ivan answers: "Are you saying that we should love *life* more than the *meaning* of it?"

"Yes," says Alyosha, "love it regardless of logic ... for then only can we grasp its meaning."

At this point, Ivan raises the question of the existence of God: "Please understand that I accept God plainly and simply. It is not God that I do not accept, but the world He has created. I do not accept God's world and I refuse to accept it."

The principal cause of Ivan's resentment against God is God's sanctioning of the horror of man's inhumanity to man and to animals. Dostoevsky was writing this passage during the Balkan War of 1878, between Russia and Turkey. Stories of Turkish atrocities, such as the nailing of prisoners to the wall by their ears before shooting them, aroused Dostoevsky's emotions to the bursting point. How can men do such things to their fellow-men? And the brutal treatment of animals — by this Dostoevsky was quite as strongly stirred. In this same chapter he repeats the scene of the *izvoschik* beating his worn-out horse to death over the head, in the same realistic manner he had used ten years earlier in *Crime and Punishment,* in Raskolnikov's dream.

"Imagine," says Ivan, "that you, Alyosha, are erecting the edifice of human destiny with the aim of making men happy in the end, but that to do this it is necessary to torture to death only one little tiny creature — would you consent to be the architect under those conditions?"

It is at this moment when Alyosha reminds Ivan of the unique figure of Christ who, because he gave his innocent blood for all and for everything, can forgive everything and everyone for everything, that Ivan replies to Alyosha in the famous chapter called "The Grand Inquisitor," which Ivan calls a *poem,* for in Russian usage, an extended parable or allegory or legend with a didactic moral purpose is called a *poem.*

— II —

It is this remarkable *poem* that D.H. Lawrence declared to be "a final and unanswerable criticism of Christ, a deadly, devastating summing up, of Dostoevsky's own opinion about Jesus. Jesus is inadequate; men must correct Him ... Christianity is in fact too difficult for men. It makes greater demands than the nature of man can bear."[26]

---

26. "Preface to Dostoevsky's The Grand Inquisitor," published 1930, 1936, 1962 in D.H. Lawrence, *Selected Literary Criticism,* New York, Viking, p. 233-41; again, in *Dostoevsky: A Collection of Critical Essays,* ed. R. Wellek, New York, Prentice-Hall, 1962, p. 91.

For my part, I consider this judgment wrongheaded, unsupported by the evidence of the text and discredited by every known fact regarding Dostoevsky's habits of thought and his uncompromising orthodoxy. With typical Marxian perversity, Lawrence fails completely to grasp the ironic intent of Dostoevsky; he takes the *poem* literally and leaves out of consideration the score of passages in the novels in which he extols Christ unreservedly. One example should convince us: "It is not as a child that I believe in Christ and profess his teaching; my hosanna has burst through a purging flame of doubts."[27] Lawrence would have us equate this declaration of religious faith with the Marxian aphorism, "Religion is the opiate of the people."

Let us look at this episode of the Grand Inquisitor in all its caustic irony. It depicts the Church in the role of Anti-Christ. The masses of humanity are portrayed as incapable of supporting the burden of their own free will. They have abandoned their will to the Church, the self-appointed guardian of their happiness. As Ivan says, "The Cardinal glories in the fact that he and his followers have at last vanquished freedom and have done so in order to make men happy."

Dostoevsky deals with this theme in terms of high and serious drama. What could possibly be more dramatic than this face-to-face confrontation of the Grand Inquisitor, fresh from the burning of heretics, spokesman for the Christian Church, challenging the meek and silent Christ

---

27. *Cf.* C. Mochulski, *op. cit.*, p. 269.

Himself, who does not deign to utter a single word throughout the long tirade of blasphemous indignities heaped upon him by the Cardinal? Yet, in spite of the profound seriousness and the intensity of the mood of this arrogant monologue, our author maintains the usual conversational pattern, with Alyosha interrupting Ivan's discourse with frequent observations; this keeps the style on a fictional level and prevents it from becoming a purely formal and didactic essay in philosophy, or a mere diatribe against religious error.

The Grand Inquisitor begins his tirade against Christ with the accusation that Christ promised that men, rebellious by nature, should be free — that he would make them free. And this freedom, which has burdened mankind for 15 centuries, they have finally abandoned — "men have handed over their freedom to us and humbly laid it at our feet." The old Cardinal "glories in the fact that he and his followers have at last vanquished freedom and have done so in order to make men happy."

At this point, Dostoevsky introduces his analysis of the human condition, using as his frame of reference the dramatic account of the temptation of Christ in the desert, told in the gospels of both Matthew and Luke (both in chapter 4) in very nearly identical words. According to St. Matthew, the Devil besought Christ to give proof of his miraculous and divine powers first, by turning the stones of the desert into bread, to which Christ answered: "Man shall not live by bread alone ..." Next, the Devil bids Christ prove his divine nature by leaping from the highest pinnacle of the temple, to be saved miraculously — if he is authentically and truly divine — by God's protecting angels. To which Christ replies: "Thou shalt not tempt the Lord thy God!" For the third temptation, the Devil offers Christ all the kingdoms of the world if he will fall down and worship him. Christ's reply: "Get thee behind me, Satan!"

Dostoevsky tells us that in these three questions the whole history of mankind is anticipated and combined in one unit, that these three images represent the insoluble, historical contradictions which everywhere human nature will encounter. Now, as the old Cardinal sees it, Christ should have accepted the Devil's challenge to turn the stones into bread:

> "...for possessed of the miraculous power to feed the masses, you would have had mankind running after you like a flock of sheep, for fear you might withdraw your hand and they would no longer have your loaves for sustenance. Instead, you rejected the Devil's offer, thinking — what sort of freedom is it if obedience is bought with loaves of bread? But in their simplicity, men cannot comprehend freedom, which they fear and dread; for nothing has ever been more unendurable to man and human society than freedom."

The end result has been that the Church has fed the masses complaining and crying out: "Feed us, for those who have promised us fire from Heaven have not given it to us! We do not mind being your slaves so long as you feed us." And they regard the priests as gods, because the priests have assumed the burden of their freedom and the responsibility for their government. For man has no greater, more constant and more agonizing anxiety than to find someone to worship, that all men can believe in, for the togetherness of worship is man's ultimate wish.

Finally, there are three positive forces able to capture and hold the conscience of mankind and keep men reasonably happy, and these three positive forces are: *Miracle, Mystery* and *Authority.* All three of these Christ rejected in casting away the Devil's three offers:

> "First you rejected the miraculous power to feed the masses; next, you destroyed the mysterious appeal of your divine nature when you refused to trust yourself to fall from the temple; and third, you respected the free-will with which man is endowed at birth and you rejected the Devil's offer of authority over them. So it is we, the Church, that have corrected your mistakes. We have united all in a common, harmonious and incontestable *ant-hill,* for the need of universal unity is the third and last torment that afflicts mankind."

The Grand Inquisitor concludes his indictment against Christ with the dramatic announcement that he will put Christ to the stake on the very next day, with the harsh observation that

> "You will behold the obedient flock which, at a mere signal from me, will rush to heap up the hot coals against the stake at which I shall burn you, because you

have come to meddle with us. For, if anyone ever deserved our fire, it is you! *Dixi!* "

Ivan seems to have finished his *poem,* but Alyosha, impatient and unsatisfied, cries out: "But it is absurd, your *poem*! In reality, it is in praise of Christ and not in his disparagement ... Your Inquisitor doesn't believe in God — and that's all his secret!"

And turning to Ivan, Alyosha blurts out: "You don't believe in God either! But how does your *poem* end?"

It is at this very point that the literary artistry of Dostoevsky achieves its finest moment. By the simple expedient of turning the tables on the hitherto dominant and arrogant old Cardinal and suddenly shifting the overwhelming mastery of the situation to the meek, humble and silent Christ, Dostoevsky creates one of the most dramatic moments in world literature — the irony of the changed situations of the two protagonists, Christ and his accuser, is magnificently impressive, for to the reader is revealed unexpectedly and in a flash of magical insight that the meek, silent, forgiving Christ is the true, the real victor in this strange confrontation between materialistic rationalism and spiritual freedom.

In a few starkly laconic sentences, Dostoevsky relates this final remarkable episode of the "Grand Inquisitor:"

"As the silent Christ looks gently into the Cardinal's flushed face, the latter approaches him, expecting some terrible and bitter answer. But Christ suddenly approached the old man and kissed him gently on his bloodless, aged lips. This was all his answer. Startled, the Cardinal moved to the door and opened it, saying: 'Go, and come no more, don't come at all — never, never!" And he let him out into the dark streets and lanes of the city. The prisoner went away."

It seems clearly evident that Dostoevsky has been presenting all along the Church as the villain in this drama; the Church, he insists, has obviously abandoned Christ's spiritual teachings for purely pragmatic, materialistic doctrines. This is the true cause of Christ's failure — the dishonest misrepresentation of his teachings by his Church. The old Cardinal knows at the end that the kiss Christ gives him is the kiss of forgiveness — the supreme irony when we recall that a moment earlier the Cardinal had threatened Christ with burning. Surely this is not, as D.H. Lawrence would have us believe, *a kiss of acquiescence,* nor is it Jesus that Dostoevsky wishes to correct. To state that the "Grand Inquisitor" is a criticism of Christ is merely wrongheaded nonsense. Rather it is a criticism of the Church and of what the institutionalized Church has made of the human condition. It constitutes the highwater mark of Dostoevsky's accomplishment both as thinker and as literary artist; had he written nothing else whatsoever, we should have to admit him to the company of the very greatest literary masters.[28]

28. Robert Lord's *Dostoevsky: Essays and Perspectives,* Univ. of California Press, 1970, 270 pp., presents much new material on theological and philosophical influences exerted upon Dostoevsky during his most prolific years. Lord applies depth psychology to the

Fittingly enough, it is Ivan, the anti-hero, the agnostic ationalist, who presents the case against the Church, iving the gloomy account of human existence without the ubstance of freedom. It is Alyosha, the youngest brother, iamed for the author's own three-year old son who died in 1878, destined for the priesthood, who refuses to accept van's conviction that "millions of God's creatures had ieen created as a mere mockery, that they would never be ible to cope with their freedom." Ivan's argument is, iowever, far and away the more convincing, and we can mly conclude that Dostoevsky was himself the Devil's nost able advocate. Who, indeed, has made a sharper inalysis of man's condition under dictatorship than this:

"We shall give them quiet happiness, the humble happiness of weak creatures, such as they were created. They will grow timid and begin looking up to us and cling to us in fear as chicks to the old mother hen. They will marvel at us and be proud that we are so mighty and so wise as to be able to tame such a rebellious and turbulent flock ... . The most tormenting secrets of their conscience they will bring to us, and we shall give them our decision ... . And they will be glad to believe our decision, because it will relieve them of their great anxiety and of their present terrible torments of coming to a free decision themselves. And

analysis of the major novels, especially his ch. XI, "Stylistics and Personality," p. 201-34; this seems to be a superior contemporary critical estimate of D.'s contribution to world literature. Edward Wasiolek gives a most useful kaleidoscopic account of the critical reception of *The Brothers Karamazov* during the past ninety years.

they will be happy, all these millions of creatures
— except the mere hundred thousand who rule over
them."

Now, who shall we suppose are the "mere hundred
thousand who rule over them?" Since 1917 and the
establishment of the closed state of Soviet Russia, with its
acolytes, many scholars have remarked upon the uncanny
anticipation of the political pattern of Communist rule in
the slogan *Miracle, mystery and authority,* which is
attributed to the old Cardinal. Who will deny that the
ascription fits equally well both Church and State wher-
ever and whenever "the mere hundred thousand" rule over
the millions hypothetically unable to cope with their
presumptive freedom?

The legend of the Grand Inquisitor is Dostoevsky's
mature and final pronouncement on the problem of free
will — the conservation of which he regarded as the
primary problem of modern civilization. It is likewise the
full and unadulterated expression of his existentialist
pessimism regarding human nature. The distance between
Ivan Karamazov and the Underground Man marks the
measure of Dostoevsky's increasing existentialist disillusionment — his growing doubt, his tortured search for
the proofs of the faith he desired so ardently to impose
upon his rational self. His own state of mind is probably
well expressed in "Ivan's Nightmare," when the Devil tells
Ivan: "Hesitations, uneasiness, the conflict between belief
and disbelief — why, this is sometimes such a torture to a
conscientious man like yourself that one would rather

hang oneself." And Ivan does indeed torment himself to the point of madness as his conscience implicates him in the murder of his wicked old father whom he hated with passionate intensity. We know, of course, that the real murderer, the wielder of the lethal weapon, was Ivan's epileptic half-brother Smerdyakov, who killed old Karamazov because "he knew Ivan, whom he greatly admired, did not like his father and perhaps desired his death."

Ivan accepts his heavy share of guilt when Smerdyakov accuses him of complicity: "You are the murderer. I was only your accomplice, your loyal page, and I done it because you told me to ... . You alone are the real murderer, though it was me what killed him." Ivan's revelation of the full truth in the presence of the presiding judge is met with complete incredulity. No one will believe Ivan's confession: "It was Smerdyakov and not my brother Dmitri who murdered my father. Smerdyakov murdered him, and I told him to do it." Ignoring Ivan's avowal of his guilt, the jury finds Dmitri guilty. This miscarriage of justice deepens the horror of this tensely dramatic tale of lust, passion and parricide.

Against the powerful forces of evil that dominate the principal action of *The Brothers Karamazov,* Dostoevsky sets up the feebly countervailing oppositon of Christian ideology in the saintly person of Father Zossima and of practical Christian virtue in the person of Alyosha Karamazov, the neophyte priest. At the end of this prodigious literary masterpiece we are informed that Ivan and Alyosha will help their condemned brother Dmitri escape to America with the regenerated prostitute Grushenka as his companion. Dmitri outlines the plan: "As soon as I arrive there with Grushenka we shall set to work.... There are still red Indians there, I'm told. Well, it's there we shall go — to the last of the Mohicans. We shall immediately apply ourselves to the study of grammar; in three years we shall learn to speak English. And as soon as we have learnt it, good-bye to America! We'll run back to Russia as American citizens... and if they recognize me, let them send me to Siberia. I don't care — it'll be just my luck!"

Quite naturally, this finale reminds us of the Siberian exile imposed upon Raskolnikov and his conversion by Sonya Marmeladov. However, Dostoevsky manages very skilfully to avoid confusing the resolution of the plots in these two novels. Grushenka is not cast in the same mould as Sonya Marmaladov; we should not believe her capable of transforming her own character, let alone to convert her lover Dmitri to the Christian faith. Moreover, Dmitri has never, like Raskolnikov, denied his religious faith; therefore he does not require conversion and there is no need for him to bear the cross of suffering since he is actually innocent of crime. On this basis, his escape to America can be condoned even by the priest Alyosha.

What Dostoevsky fails to clear up for us is the fate of Ivan. In the novel his last spoken words were uttered from the witness stand at the trial, when the jury has committed the juridical error of condemning the innocent Dmitri as the murderer of his father. "Why," shouts Ivan, "why is everything in the world so stupid?" We may assume, I think, that his strong feeling of guilt for his assumed complicity in his father's murder will ultimately guide him o conversion; but Dostoevsky leaves both him and us as well in ambiguous perplexity. It is probable that Dostoevsky identified himself with Ivan, whose destiny he could not disclose because he was not prepared to predict the outcome of his own personal struggle with uncertainty and doubt.[29]

Indeed, there is some sentient part of Dostoevsky himself in all his multitude of fictional characters and it is this extraordinary empathic climate with which he surrounds his personages that gives them the air of living beings. He seems to share their anxieties, their doubts are his doubts, their vices are his vices, their rare moments of greatness are also his. More so, perhaps, than any other writer before or since, he possessed the mysterious faculty of distilling the quintessence of himself in the process of putting words upon a page of writing-paper. And what other artist has experienced so intensely and to the same degree the shattering machinations of the demon of existence? His life was surely far stranger than his fiction, and this strangeness seems to have entered mysteriously into the community of bizarre personages that constitute his image of human society. First for himself, and then for all of us who read his books, he discovered the primary importance of the contingent and accidental event — the most trifling action, the most trifling utterance — in the overall pattern of the individual destiny. It seems to have been his special and peculiar mission to turn our gaze away

29. Irving Howe has observed that Dostoevsky wished every man to be Christ, that this simple heretical concept, which denies the usefulness of the Church, is the very essence of his religious thinking; *Politics and the Novel*, New York, 1957; p. 56.

from what he called "the image of some sort of impossible generalized man," to concentrate our attention upon our particular personal existence.[30] Here again, Dostoevsky anticipated one of the fundamental tenets of Existentialist analysis as this has been developed over the past century

Often enough, Dostoevsky's views on political society appear quite anachronistic, reactionary and even unnecessarily subservient to the always suspicious authorities of the czarist regime. During the last ten years of his life (1871-1881), Dostoevsky was on terms of intimate acquaintanceship with K.P. Pobedonostsev, member of the Imperial Council and later procurator-general to the Holy Synod. Through this official's good offices, Dostoevsky met leading members of the czar's cabinet, the higher military and influential members of the nobility, with whom he exchanged ideas, formal visits and views on political questions. In his *Memoirs*, Pobedonostsev, that prodigy of political and religious reaction, claimed that his novelist friend had conceived the character of Father Zossima according to his suggestions. It was Pobedonostsev who arranged the impressive state funeral of the author whose reputation he had established as "the most distinguished conservative writer of the century."[31]

Dostoevsky rejected altogether science and technology that new culture which he referred to in *The Underground Man* as the "Crystal Palace of man's illusions and enslavement." Yet it was this self-same author who presented in his two greatest novels, *The Possessed* and *The Brothers*

30. *Vide supra*, V. Saduro, *op. cit.*, p. 240.
31. R.F. Byrnes, *op. cit.*, p. 95.

Karamazov, the most astonishingly accurate blue-print of the socio-political events of our present scientific century — the conquest of violent, revolutionary Marxism and the pattern of Communist dictatorship over the larger half of mankind. Likewise, in his search for the psychological self and the emotional resources of the primary physical body, Dostoevsky anticipated the tendency of our present time.

Today, the question is often raised, "What has happened to the novel; what is wrong with the novel?" From the example of the Grand Inquisitor a partial answer suggests itself. Too many contemporary novelists have abandoned almost completely what was the paramount practice of the nineteenth-century masters. They have rejected the dynamic exaltation of the willful temperament in their fictional personages; they choose to depict — exhaustively and exhaustingly — frustrated, do-nothing eccentrics or shrinking prodigies of implausibility. This transformation of the novel genre has been noted and intelligently explained by Norman Mailer: "Realistic literature never caught up with the rate of change in American life. Indeed, it had fallen further behind, and the novel gave up any desire to be a creation equal to the phenomenon of the country itself; it settled for being a metaphor."[32] What happened in America was duplicated in varying degree the world over.

Forty years ago the Soviet critic Bakhtin revealed quite accurately the secret of Dostoevsky's originality as a writer:

---

32. Cited from *Saturday Review of Literature* (12/ 28/ '68), p. 30.

"His originality lay in his ability to form an artistically objective conception of his character and to project these characters as entirely independent entities, without having to resort to lyricism or to insert his own voice among theirs. At the same time, he managed to avoid constricting them within a circumscribed psychological reality.... It is enough for someone to appear on Dostoevsky's horizon for the author's concept of him to become an incarnated force in the process of realizing its own personality."[33]

As a matter of fact, Dostoevsky was well versed in philosophic writings, both European and Russian; "yet he never set out to be a philosopher; instead, he used the materials of philosophy and of ideas to construct the mental and spiritual world of his characters."[34] Surely there is ample justification of the Existentialist claim that Feodor Mikhailovitch Dostoevsky was in spirit as well as in practice a precursor, possibly even one of the founding fathers of modern Existentialism.

With this primary question thus perfunctorily answered in the affirmative, it is natural to ask whether Dostoevsky was consciously aware of his identification with this unorthodox approach to the problems of philosophy. We have to remember that Dostoevsky was first of all a professional writer, who made his living as a writer of

---

33. M.M. Bakhtin, *Problemy tvorchestva Dostoevskago* (Problem Connected with Dostoevsky's Creative Work), Leningrad, 1929; p 43.

34. *Ibidem*, p. 191, as Englished by Lord, *op. cit.*, p. 202.

iction. In his writing there is no evidence anywhere that
ıe felt himself to be a participant in any special *école* or
movement, once the early attraction to socialist ideas had
disappeared during the exile. We know that he read avidly
Dickens and Balzac and many other writers of fiction
- even Eugène Sue, the serialist of *Les Mystères du Peuple*.
However, he certainly had no knowledge of the writings of
his Danish contemporary Kierkegaard, nor does he men-
tion the words *existential, existentialism* or *existentialist*
anywhere in any of his own writings. Yet these terms were
already in current usage in the 1830's and '40's, among
those familiar with Hegel's philosophy; for Hegel had
introduced the terms with the intention of denying the
fact. We know that Hegel's ideas were much discussed
among the Russian student groups and especially by the
coterie of writers who accepted Belinsky as their leader.
We may speculate that, as a member of this group,
Dostoevsky was to some extent, at least, cognizant of
Hegelianistic ideas. But there is no evidence that he was led
to adopt existential points of view because of any dislike
of Hegel's own rejection of them, as was the case with
Kierkegaard.[35]

It appears, rather, that Dostoevsky reached his existentialist views quite independently, as it were by accident,
entirely from his accumulated observations of human
existence, including his own deeply tragic life. His views

35. Robert Lord, *op. cit.*, p. 202. Lord indicates the significant
similarities in thinking among the philosophers and writers of
Dostoevsky's generation, despite the absence of direct communication or awareness of the spontaneity of their common interests.

were very much his own. How amazed this literary genius would be were he to know that he is hailed as the prophet of modern Existentialism by the Christian, the secular and the atheistic-agnostic exponents alike! Can there by any doubt that Dostoevsky was firmly attached to the Christian camp of Existentialist thought? We have shown that four of his five major novels conclude upon a Christian Existentialist *dénouement*. What would he think if he knew that the avowed atheists — Sartre, Camus and many other famous novelists of today and yesterday – have hailed Dostoevsky as their true precursor?

Finally, it ought to be emphasized that Dostoevsky's existentialism is in no sense systematic, nor formally or technically philosophical. He has indeed inspired several professional philosophers, but as for himself, he remains on the purely literary level. This is partly, of course, a matter of style. His novels are certainly more closely related to pure philosophy than any other fiction of his time. It may even be true that Existentialism is in fact irreducible to formal systematic philosophy in the traditional pattern; there are many who hold that it has not yet reached that stage. Meanwhile, thanks to the genius of Dostoevsky, we have its simplest, its clearest and its most eloquent expression.